POEMS From Under The EGG

Harvey O'Leary

Copyright© 2021 Harvey O'Leary
ISBN: 978-81-8253-784-2

First Edition: 2021
Rs. 200/-

Cyberwit.net
HIG 45 Kaushambi Kunj, Kalindipuram
Allahabad - 211011 (U.P.) India
http://www.cyberwit.net
Tel: +(91) 9415091004
E-mail: info@cyberwit.net

No part of this book may be reproduced or transmitted in any form or by
any means, electronic, mechanical, photocopying, or otherwise, without
the express written consent of Harvey O'Leary.

Contents

I

TWO FRAGMENTS

There is an island lost at sea
Far from the shores of the Bay of Capri.
It has no songs or poetry,
No place in mythology,
Too small to figure in history.
It can only be…

Under the Egg, outside the town of Xanthi,
You left the white road for the olive trees
And heard the howling of the wolves in the mountains
And louder, closer, the incessant chirping of crickets in the grass.
On the vine stalk, black grapes hung in bunches
As big and succulent as plums for you to eat.
You wetted your finger, wiped the dust from a grape,
Plucked it from the vine…
                    …shaking his fist,
Angry at the trespass and the theft,
You turned away. He shouted after you.
When you looked back, wanting to protest,
The old man was jabbing at his eye,
Telling you that he had seen what you'd done.

EMPORIUM

The Sea Gate
The twin peaks smoke above Colonia.
Beyond the rows of vine and olive trees
And the large villas on the mountain slope
The bay water glimmers in the noon heat.
White sails of seaward vessels disappear
In the glare of the sun. Business is good.
For the traders in the forum life has
Returned to a profitable routine.
In the shade of the plane trees in the square
A bustling, noisy crowd of porters,
Advertisers, fabric sellers, teachers,
Mule drivers, doctors ply their different trade.
The inns are full of rowdy customers
Arguing over the toss, shuffling dice,
Cracking a joke about the public baths
And the patrons running out into the street
When the ground opened and the walls collapsed
And the whole Earth shook with seismic laughter.

Hortus

In a garden at the heart of the house,
Where the family gives thanks to Venus,
Birdsong should be heard and water trickling
Softly, for this is a refuge of peace
And stillness, opulence and luxuriance.
The air should be cool here, plant and water
Give some respite from the late August heat.
Near the family shrine, the old domino
Reclines asleep on his marble cushioned couch.
Standing behind him, a Greek slave raises
And lowers a fan to cool the broiling air.

In the Room of the Mysteries

Hidden, out of ear-shot, in flickering
Torchlight, priestess, domina and her attendants
Perform the ancient rites. The torch flames
Burn under the blood-red frescoes' friezes.
Shadow and flickering light lend movement
To the group of figures in the room and
On the walls. The wedding preparations.
The slow procession to the alter.
The plate of cakes. The olive branch offered.
The priestess crowned with an olive reed.
The three dancing faun. The woman in Greek
Attire. A veil lifted. A whip raised.
The smiling satyr and the unplucked lyre.
The annihilation of a goddess.
The death of a mother and the birth of a child.
On bended knees the birth of a mad god.

A TABLE ON THE BEACH

Covered entirely in white cloth
With neither top nor legs showing
The table looks curiously dressed.

At the four corners stand four chairs,
Evenly spaced, backs ramrod straight:
Four soldiers awaiting inspection.

Medusa, sea anemone,
Fixed to a rock or floating free,
Dances alone for everything
Is subject to its savage sting.
Still and transparent as water
The shrimp doesn't move a whisker,
But waits, a patient water cat
Set to pounce on a water rat.
The crab never one to settle,
Readies for defence or battle;
In movement seems to dodge and flee
An invisible enemy.
Can a starfish really be
A living breathing entity?
It looks more like a water toy,
The play thing of a girl or boy.
Sea horse merely drifts with the tide.
Climb on its back and take a ride.
You will go nowhere for the fish
Moves with the purpose of a wish.

Goldfish looking out of their bowl
Believe that they would have the whole
World to swim in could they but pass
Through the harder water of glass.

The grilled fish is recommended
But the waiter suggests the guests
Might first like to have an hors d'oeuvre.

In the centre of the table
A candle's black flame flickers
On silverware and bone china.

IN THE WAKE OF THE STORM

Wind sweeps across the dunes and falls,
Sprinkling a little sand;
Undisturbed, the petrified grass
Crowns the crest of the strand.

A buried chair of driftwood shows
Four broken, sunken legs;
Tossed by the tide, stones round and smooth
Like scattered cuckoos' eggs.

A pile of neatly folded clothes
Close to the rising sea,
Where nestle coins and keys and rings
And coral jewellery.

The sea's huge shoal of random coins
Glitters gold and silver,
Shines in the eye and spills from the chest
Of the abandoned swimmer.

II

PHINEAS

The uncapped bottle's sudden *shhhhh*
  In a large crowded room:
Contents flow and glasses are raised
  To toast the bride and groom.

Outside, the mood is sombre.
  The day is dressed in black.
Crowds move in a slow procession,
  Taking a well-worn track:

A funeral or a marriage,
  It rains down on the dead
While clouds, like cheering guests above,
  Shower the newly-wed.

Wake or revels? What does it matter?
  You go with all the rest
Though lagging behind a little –
  The uninvited guest.

NARCISSUS

You join the dots of the scattered stars.
   You die and then give birth.
You put the face of the man on the moon
   To look back down on Earth.

You fall asleep… and asleep awake to
   The face of another,
And then you regard your reflection as
   Lover would a lover.

 In empty space there's no reply
   But you can hear an echo.
The features of the man you see
   Are always more than shadow.

You cross the cold mountains of the moon.
   You cross the sunless sea.
You cross… and arrive to tell the tale
   With lunar authority.

FURIES

1. Corpus

No shadow darkened that face,
Lengthened that frown:
Out of what disgust, disgrace,
You chose to drown,
    Cry, *Let the Earth turn to stone;*
Let the fires burn.

But first, let us play with flesh,
So taut and keen,
So astonishingly fresh,
Packed, stacked, and lean.
    Let us see the skeleton:
Unwrap the bone!

11. Nerves

A steel pen teases the tissue
    Of the alert brain.
You witness the operation,
    Experience no pain,
Guide the hand of the surgeon,
    Who doesn't complain.

The skull cap neatly refitted,
    You rise and then you walk.
Once discharged and recovered
    You can (with your talk)

Reproduce *La Giaconda*,
    Using a stick of chalk.

111. Animus

Why does the angler take exception
To fish being killed by pollution;
State his open condemnation
At the wanton decimation?

For had the fish taken his bait
They would be dead, at any rate.

——-

You, men of ideas,
Conduct in your study,
Against a battered body,
A case for the cleaver
In the act of slaughter.

The animals outside
Can make no more defence
(In unholy alliance)
Then judge the treachery
Of a dog's loyalty.

——-

So then, on land or out at sea,
In a court of wilderness,
Do you expect fidelity
When you meet your nemesis?

THE BIRTH OF SKULL EGG

I. *Skull Effigy*

The frozen seas, the petrified waves,
Gave birth to me amongst watery graves.

I am Skull Egg. I am carcass and rock,
The mineral bone and the fleshy sock.

I hang suspended. I am the hanger
To hold and stretch a piece of leather.

I am the glove that will slip from the hand.
I am the flesh that will slip from the bone.

I am the uncountable grains of sand.
I am the unbreakable, matchless stone.

I wear the colours of yellow and white
To ruffle the blue and ward off the night,

To say, *I am no one*, in all but name.
I am the blood that is banged in the brain.

The moon is no mouth; the sun is no eye.
I am the bruise that discolours the sky.

I am the cries from the mouth when the skin
Is picked and pierced and peeled away.

I am the grimace, the face on display,
As the fingers press and are pushed within.

...

Commemorate me with a bust of bone:
So difficult to render flesh in stone.

II. *The House of Skull Egg*

The doors are locked
But if you were to enter my house
You would find six unfurnished rooms.
The doors to these rooms can only be unlocked
With one of three keys
Made of glass, of ivory, and of steel.

In the first room
There is nothing
But light cords of various length
Dangling from the ceiling,
And, propped against the wall, a ladder
In the shape of a staircase.

In the second, an electric fan
Lying on its back, blades a-whirring,
Which is surprising

For though the cord
Reaches to the wall
It isn't plugged in.

In the third, a kind of aviary
Of different species, rare delicacies,
All of them strangely indolent
As though the desire for flight, for singing
And squawking, had long since
Flown away.

In the fourth room hang
My coats of leather
From hooks in the shape of bent fingers.
They soak and drip
And basins on the floor
Collect the weeping.

In the fifth room, nailed to the walls,
Bright gleaming shapes of steel,
Pointed and serrated,
While, in a corner, leaning together,
Hoe and rake, pick and spade,
And the other tools of my trade.

In the sixth and final room
There is everything but
A white-draped pedestal
On which a telephone rests
And is ringing eternally.

III. *The Counsel of Skull Egg*

A song, a song, I am singing.
O do not fear, my friend,
For death is not the beginning.
Death is merely the end.

A race, a race, I am running.
My friend, no need to run,
Standing on the finishing line,
Holding the starter's gun.

A life, a life, I am living
(A truth to tell a lie).
My friend, the only way to live
Is to prepare to die.

IV. *The Riddle of Skull Egg*

Do you wish to speak to me,
Stranger? For I can be
A good friend
And
An even better enemy.

Can you give me an answer
To the old familiar
Question?
Come,
You will leave me none the wiser.

V. *The Bounty of Skull Egg*

Come, join my company of one.
Take this gift of a loaded gun.
Make a wish; then blow out the sun.

Together alone we will dare
Prick a balloon and free the air.
You have *everything* to declare.

Now, look beyond what you can see,
Beyond the limits they decree:
Your target is eternity.

To what do you most aspire?
Point the gun a little higher:
Crosshairs in the line of fire.

Careful, an invisible race
Do battle in the air for space.
(A second death may grant them grace.)

Careful because a single blast
May well turn out to be your last,
And you will join that wretched cast.

VI. *Nest Egg*

The first-born nestling hatched:
A clutch of eggs dispatched.

The air thick with the seed
Of the indignant weed.

Moth and butterfly snub
The long-forgotten grub.

Flocks journey to the house
Abandoned by a mouse.

Enmity of the rat
Breeds in the sullen cat.

A snake maintains a grin,
Shedding its second skin.

Eyes of the floating fly
Multiply… multiply... multiply.

Soft walls of the red flower
Slowly close to devour.

To win and lose at snap
In the carnivore's trap.

PROTEUS

Counting the many to be fed,
You hold in your hands a piece of bread:
Host to the spots that turn its white
Into the blues and greens of blight.

In this secret consecration
You celebrate the transformation
Of fungus, virus, tumour and spore,
Armies to feast on a running sore.

GORGON

The temperature drops below absolute zero.
Winter arrives earlier than spring.
Days end with something less and greater than night.

In the half-light, clock hands are fixed in a smile.
Compass needles point to imaginary poles.
Life slows down to keep company with stone.

. . .

Stone is the *ovum* and the *mala* of stasis
Until in the sky, in a mess of yellows and whites,
From the sun's spilt yolk you slowly arise -

Heralded by the silence, rise, like the dawning
Of a new planet to a new meridian,
Then slowly revolve to show your unmasked face.

. . .

Your crown, a nest of hissing vicious glory
Of bird-like creatures, winged but featherless,
Rooted to the spot though poised to fly.

Bunched together, these querulous siblings,
Identical yet constantly at war,
Would rather perish than look you in the eye.

TAURUS

'… ego vel Prochytam praepono Suburae;
nam quid tam miserum, tam solum vidimus, ut non
deterius credas horrere incendia, lapsus
tectorum absiduous ac mille pericula saevae
urbis et Augusto recitantes mense poetas?'

Juvenile Satire Three, 1. 4-9

Inspecting a parade of graves
For signs of life, you came upon
An epitaph to raise the spirits
After morale had been undone.

Inscribed in stone, it simply read:
Here lies one, who may be nowhere.
Thus to citations for the dead,
The oath of an agnostic soldier.

MYTHOS

Where does the ocean cross the sea?
Where does one give way to the other?
Where is the end to fluency?
Show us Mediterranean water.

Rifles trained on an empty sky
Point to the bullets' trajectory
With lines that are unrecorded by
The pages of a desert diary.

VERSE AND SUBVERSE

The patter of tiny feet,
Tiny, tiny feet
That could paddle in a thimble
And be wiped with a stamp.

The stone cutter tapped
The blunt end of his chisel
To make the sharp end
Cut into the stone.

These lines, these lines, I'm reciting,
And so much more to say.

So gentle are the contours of the land
You think the country flat.
You hardly feel the gradient
Beneath your climbing feet.

Out of imagination
Surely will come
Godhead or devil
To be worshipped or spat on.
Mankind cannot bear a vacuum
For very long.

You, on the sideline, with the other fools
Who have to be reminded of the rules
Which would make a difference if they could only see
The ball chasing players chased by the referee.

The cries of tactics and the cries of pain
To ignorant ears seem to be much the same.

Does the sea anemone
Wave its long arms to you and me?
No, for the arms will wave until
The current is completely still.

Tread carefully
For they rest precariously.

The driveway to the house rises and winds capriciously.
You go. You come.
You may find yourself back where you started.

Sponges swell and soak the seas dry.
Rain-drenched clouds fall out of the sky.

The Sun…the Sun.
I do not care for the Sun.
The Sun can go and burn.

The bottle washed up on the shore
Turned out to be a Russian doll.

The sun fizzles out, and the moon
Is popped like a party balloon.

Discover if the caged bird really sings.
In the garden shed you will find
All that you need.

At dusk, smouldering, smoking… amber, ochres… embers…
Pink, white clouds drift.

INNAMORATO, INNAMORATA

Rain-saturated clouds
Hang in the sky like enormous boulders.
Innamorato, Innamorata,
The moon is larger than usual.
It is a stranger standing uncomfortably close, so close
That you can almost feel its breath.
What does it want from you that you are not prepared to give it,
Or wants to give you that you can't accept.

It is an obstinate presence.

You wish it would stand back.
You wish it would withdraw.
You wish it would just go away.
But the moon doesn't move.
Instead, it challenges you with its blank unflinching stare.
Daring you to speak.
Daring you not to speak.
Daring you to reveal everything it already knows.

Innamorato, a la luna,
In time, or out of time,
The moon wanes, leaves the stage,
And you regret its departure.
It is the loss of the company of a stranger.
For what remains but the pinprick
Of absent stars,
The nullity of the sun,
And, beyond

Ghostly other worlds,
Skeins and nets,
Whipped clouds of greens and yellows and reds
Flung into space,
Gust and vapours.

      …

Does the slipper, once outside the house, turn
Into a shoe?
I wonder
For the rocking horse goes everywhere and nowhere.
Innamorato, Innamorata.
Hold aloft your black umbrella
In order to remain
On the wire, high and tight.

Innamorato, Innamorata.
Dancer and spinning top
Spin endlessly,
Releasing
A flock of feathers,
A whirlwind of birds, a unicorn
That gallops into the deepest wood.
Innamorato, Innamorata

Innamorato, dura mater.
The umbrella that you hold
Is a bats' secret conclave.
Do they confer? Do they decide?
When you visit the cave of a shoe
You'll find a clutch of speckled eggs
In a small brown water nest.

Innamorato, alma mater,
Under the ruck of black wings,
You will uncover
A flock of birds and bats
Nestling together,
One on top of another,
Among the cracked eggs
And tufts of hair and feather.

...

On a blasted hill
Sitting bare-footed,
You inspect
The nails of your feet and your hands.
They show such neglect that you ask
To see the root, buried deep in the cuticle,
And in reply,
As if in a dream,
Rise
Great whorls of tusk
From fingers and toes
And spread outward
Then turn
Back on themselves
Like daggers
To pierce the flesh and the organs,
To run through the neck and the back and the head
To emerge out of the legs, the armpits and the eyes
To sink into the ground
And hold you in a cage, a coffin of nails,
Or rise
And again spread

Like great antlers, like leafless branches
On which your flesh is skewered and bloody.

The building has collapsed
Dust floats in the air
All that remains
All that now stands
Buffeting the wind
Is a gable wall
And a high window
In which a figure
Breaks clear of the surface
The arms raised
The neck strained
And the face
The face turning, twisted
Held in place
By the glass stained.

III

THE SPIRIT OF THE GAME

Solitaire

No different if you cheat
Or play fair –
Always end up losing
At solitaire.

The game depends on how
Much choice you allow.
You deal the cards and play
Them just as they lay.

This is no
Game of Tarot.

A game for one player.
The aim – to match a pair.
With all the pairs taken,
Shuffle, deal again.

This is no
Game of Tarot.

You don't have a partner.
You are the sole player.
You play the game alone.
You are on your own.

This is no
Game of Tarot.

Cube

To wake each day
In the same space
In the same silence
Resting against one
Of six white walls
In a room where

You keep company
With cordless machines,
Toys and mirrors,

Collected, unsorted
Lying in a heap
At your broken feet.

A cube of ice would do for dice.

To wake each night
In the same orbit
On the same station

Where the sun sets
And the moon rises
And you believe

Pointing beyond
With old fingers
In which old bones

Are shuffled and rolled
To a table, a bowl
Of ice and water.

A FEW LINES ONLY

In recognition of the routine,
The well-oiled predictable machine,
The words which say no more than you mean,

Instead of the days you recall when you
Were far from the corridor and the queue,
The effort to order something new.

THE TERRACE

None so different as to be
Outstanding. Yet none exactly
The same. The terraced houses stand
As a testament to neighbours

Who will always find something in
Common when they meet each other
Over the fence or at the gate
Or in cars parked further down the street.

NO SOONER SAID

You declare, you unburden, you reason:
Your conscience is perfectly clear,
But before you move on to the next thing
The words want a word in your ear:

Yes, I am sure that it must have meant something
To the listener with bated breath
And the one with the passive expression
Of the stoic awaiting death,

And the others who nod in agreement
Or signal they've got what was said.
But you will have understood nothing
If you let all this go to your head.

You coax, you encourage, you finish,
Announce that the session is through,
But for someone it's only beginning
Because now it is all about you.

SUMMERTIME

Buildings

High walls topped with scrolls of barbed wire
flying scraps of black refuse bags, a scarf,

a tie. Main gates padlocked, chain hanging
Like a loose belt, and lock hanging heavily

as a stone. No signs are needed here
to keep you out. No signs are needed here.

Across the empty yard, frosted windows
are barred or shuttered. No movement in the hall,

hallway, stairs, stairway, corridors,
library, laboratories, classrooms.

Outside, the caretaker's lodge stands deserted.
A solitary bicycle is chained

to a steel hoop. But beyond the yard
and school buildings in overgrown pitches

rise the giant 'H' of enormous goalposts
through which a ball, like a bird, once flew.

The Crossing

The heat. The orange globes on either side
of the crossing seem to burn brighter

in the heat. Where is the lollypop lady
with her blue peaked cap and spotless white coat,

standing statue-still in the middle of the road
to see her charge safely across? Elsewhere

perhaps dreaming of another September,
with legs too weary, with back too stiff,

with arms too old to hold outstretched
the sign now at her side. The lights flicker,

threatening to go out forever.
Do you remember the lollypop lady

who holds in her hands the pages
of another contract soon to expire?

Plenty

In the greengrocers the unsold fruit rots,
despite the draughts of liquidated air,

despite the neat rows of separate trays
and the labelled exotica, and cut-

price on a huge over-ripe abundance.
Even the staple fails to sell: apples

oranges, bananas, lemons, grapes,
stock out of season and over-seas.

The apples boil in the heat; the green
stew at the same rate as the red; the pears

lose their soft shape; the lemon coloured oranges
slowly deflate, as do the clusters

of wrinkly-skinned grapes, punnets of currant,
date, prune and fig, pouches of vinegar.

…

The till is empty. The name over
the shop door almost unrecognisable.

The intense heat, a disinterested crowd,
a 'For Sale' sign further down the street

distract the grocer for a while. He dawdles
outside, seems to know no one, mutters

to himself, 'Who will buy with the trays
So full and the price of goods much cheaper

Elsewhere?' Slowly, he counts the day's takings.
Like the weather the competition here

has proven too hot. Soon he must surrender,
and go, and be a grocer no longer.

DREAM PERFORMANCE

'For my next trick, all I need is a table and a chair,'
The conjuror announced.
'The stable table which has remained
Since the dawn of time *unchanged.*'
The audience were unimpressed.
The conjuror smiled, nodded to the Gods, and behind him
The lights slowly came up
On two things covered with white sheets,
One looked like a chair and the other, a table.
'It's only a chair – nothing but a chair!' someone shouted.
'Yes, it *is* a chair,' replied the conjuror,
'But a *unique* chair, a remarkable chair, a chair
The like of which has never been seen.'
And, before the audience could dismiss his claim,
He pulled the cover away
To reveal a perfectly ordinary wooden chair
With
Its front legs crossed,
Which made it look almost human.
The conjuror snapped his fingers
And the chair uncrossed its legs.
He wriggled his fingers, sprinkling invisible magic dust,
And it went up on one hind leg
Like a ballerina,
Revolved, hopped a little about the stage,
Tapping a secret code of its own;
Then, deciding its turn was about done
And not one to outstay its welcome,

Exited, still hoping on one leg,
To the audience's astonishment and dismay.

Now it was the turn of the table.
The lights dimmed, an unseen drum rolled,
The conjuror crossed to the table, took the edges
Of the large white drape in both hands
And, teasing the audience, slowly, ever so slowly, pulled it away
To reveal nothing but a perfectly ordinary kitchen table.
The magician raised his hand,
Reminded the audience of the magical chair.
They settled, and, despite the odd rumble of discontent, waited…
And waited…and then
As their patience was about to give way
Something begin to stir
Inside the table.
Commanded by the conjuror,
The table began to climb off the ground,
Up it rose
To cheering and thunderous applause,
Then settled
In mid air
Directly above the conjuror.
He acknowledged the audience's response
With both arms outstretched.

And that would have been it.
The performance would have been over
But for the table
Which suddenly buckled,
Slipped
From its perch and came
Crashing down

On the head of the man
On the stage.
The laughter, the cheering, the applause
Died.
The table, having landed on its legs, rocked from side to side
Above the outstretched body of the conjuror,
Then, as if furious by the response,
It suddenly split asunder,
Cracked open,
Shooting into the air
Shards of crockery, splinters of glass, a flash of silver,
Cutlery's
Gleaming weaponry,
Which, like a shower of arrows, flew
Over the heads of the baffled orchestra
Into the panic-stricken auditorium.

THE CHICANE

You awoke
On the sandy shore in the cold light,
In the dreamtime,
Singing your world into existence,
Aranda, Aranda,
And the sand twinkled with a million eyes.
You were then silenced
For the cacophony of the waves,
The drifting tide and the falling rain
Gave rise to sea music
No instrument could play, no voice sing,
To herald the arrival
Out of the sea
Of a vision so incredible
Your heart did battle
With your ribs.
Shrouded in sea mist, in the blues and whites of the air,
The figure hovered in the air
Above where you lay
And so to this audience
You sang the sea into existence.

A long time ago there was much
Less water than there is today;
Yet the water teemed with so much
Life that it would take forever
To count. Water was so happy;
It couldn't keep still, but moved
About ceaselessly, flowed and ebbed,
Sprung and fell back upon itself

With the delight of a dolphin.
One day, however, a quarrel
Broke out among the animals
Which, hitherto, had lived in peace.
A fierce struggle ensued until
Finally the defeated
Were driven out onto the land.
The water was so upset that
It burst into floods of salty tears.
Centuries were to pass before
The water ceased to cry, and by
Then much of the Earth's surface
Was covered with its weeping.
Sorrow gave way to anger as
The water felt bereft of its
Creatures. Its waves lashed at the land,
Great whirlwinds rose out of its depths
Scattering storm clouds that rained down
On the Earth; rivers and lakes
Swollen with rain flooded their banks;
Geysers sprung from under the ground.
And the vast bodies of water,
The seas and the oceans, rolled
And roll landward, to reclaim all
That has been lost. Water knows that
One day it will succeed and all
The creatures that were taken
Will once again live in its depths.

The riddle of the light and mist
Present a double, man or woman,
The whiskered chin, the wrinkled breast,
Ugly because once beautiful,
Who holds aloft a black umbrella.

Wings of a bat stitched together.
The pelt of a lamb about its throat,
The bloody carcass at its feet.

The tilted umbrella sends
Shadows back across its face,
Drawn like curtains to reveal
A weeping yellow jaundiced eye
And the yellows of bone and teeth
And a touch of red at the lips
For in the corner of the mouth
Wagging, as from a piece of fruit,
The wriggling blind worm of tongue.

The spotlight of a harvest moon
Shines on the stage of a lagoon
Where larvae rises to the surface,
To a floating piece of pumice
Which drifts away to colonise
Other wrecks from the wreck that lies
On the reef bed. Now, leave the sea
To crab and sea anemone,
To grey shark feeding near the shore,
Polyp and sponge stuck to the floor,
To seaweed drifting in the current,
To coral's growing monument,
To its white skeleton of stone
For now the lunar cycle's done.

Leave the coral to its colony;
Leave the shallow, moon-lit water;
Go and live far, far from the sea,
And at low tide even farther.

LEAVES

The leaf on the twig
Of the tree that is felled
Still stirs in the wind.

The surface a ripple,
Rippling with falling water,
Strives to recover.

Limp, wet with streaming spray,
Leaves hang over the water
Like drops of water.

Leaf-upon-leaf fall,
Falling, floating, flying, fashion
Speckled mobile space.

Gone, everything gone.
The trees' sudden flurry of leaves,
Like rain, like bare-branched grief.

A branch, clustered with leaves,
Leaning out, straight as a rod,
Challenges the air.

These precious leaves…
How we cut our fingers
On their sharp edges.

But let the leaves settle
For they have been gathered
Into a loose pile.

The door is opening
And the pages of a book
Flutter a little.

THE FROG AND THE GRASSHOPPER

The frog had spent his days in the forest,
And never ventured far from the river
Except to hunt. This way of life had not
Altered much when one day he happened
To meet a grasshopper. The grasshopper,
Too, had never been outside the forest
And was eager to know what lay beyond.
'Let us journey together,' suggested
The frog, and the grasshopper readily
Agreed. First, they built a boat, intending
To sail down the river, but the grasshopper
Refused to get into it. 'I'm sorry
But I have never been on the water.
I'm afraid we'll sink.' For him the river
Was as deep and as wide as the ocean.
'Never mind,' said the frog. 'If you wish, we can
Travel through the forest, though the journey
Will take much longer… Come let us go now.'
They set off into the trees, soon losing
The sound of the old familiar river.
At first, they moved quickly and easily,
The forest floor was much the same as that
By the riverbank, the vegetation
Presenting no obstacles. Gradually,
However, it began to grow thicker,
And the animals had to pick their way
Slowly and with difficulty.
The frog grew tired. The grasshopper tried to
Keep his spirits up by imagining

What it would be like outside the forest.
The frog never thought that he would make it.
He complained that the forest seemed to grow
Darker as they moved outward. He wanted
To return to his home by the river but
The grasshopper insisted they continue.
Eventually, they believed they were
Making progress as the number of trees
Grew fewer and fewer, the grass thicker.
Then, in a burst of sunlight, they were clear
Of the forest. A vast plain without trees
Or grass or animals lay before them.
The frog and the grasshopper cheered loudly.
What new world were they set to discover?
With renewed energy the moved on, looking
Back, now and again, to see how far they'd come.

…

But they hadn't got far when they
Came to a sudden halt. Ahead of them
Rose a fence that stretched across the plain
As far as the eye could see. The only way
Forward was to climb over the top, which
The grasshopper attempted to do but
Fell back down to earth for the fence
Was as smooth as a sheet of glass. The frog
Leaped into the air and came within
Inches of reaching the top before he
Too fell back down and landed with
A bump next to his companion. 'If I
Were to climb onto the back of the frog,'
Thought the grasshopper, 'and were he to make
The same jump, I could then leap from his back

Onto the top of the fence.' The grasshopper
Waited till the frog had fallen asleep
Before putting his plan into action.
He sat perfectly still on the frog's back,
Not daring to move least he disturb him.
Finally the frog woke. It was almost
Daybreak. He called out. There was no answer.
He looked around but the grasshopper was
Nowhere to be seen. Believing he was alone
And that his companion had left him, he
Decided to head back to the forest.
But a voice whispered, 'Frog, do not go.
Try jumping over the fence one last time.
You will never succeed unless you try.'
The frog, thinking he had nothing to lose,
Crouched low in the grass, summoned all his strength,
And, on the count of three, shot into the air.
Up he sailed, his long legs dangling beneath
Him. Up he went reaching further than
Before and, when he finally arrived
At the crest of his ascent, the grasshopper
Leapt from his back onto the top
Of the wall. From there, with the rising sun
Pouring light across the land, the insect
Surveyed the world beyond. 'O frog, if you
Were able to see what I see…' His eyes
Misted over. He could no longer speak.
He looked down to where the frog sat, still
As a stone, in the shadow of the wall.
He called to him but there was no reply.
He looked out again across the land, and
Then down at the ground on the other side.
There was no going back.